# Executive Transitions 2

Leveraging Experience For Future Success!

by

Thomas F. Casey Jr.
Managing Principal
Discussion Partner Collaborative

**TP**™

**TELEMACHUS PRESS**

Cover art and designed by Telemachus Press, LLC

Published by Telemachus Press, LLC
http://www.telemachuspress.com

Visit the author's website:
http://www.discussionpartners.com

ISBN: 978-1-948046-61-9 (eBook)
ISBN: 978-1-948046-62-6 (Paperback)

Version 2019.04.23

# Testimonials

Having spent the majority of my career in executive management in non-profit organizations, I well understand the challenges inherent in shifting between sectors, whether from for-profit to non-profit or vice-versa. Transition Planning is pivotal to successfully navigating the on- and off-ramps between enterprises. I began working with Tom Casey when he was with The Concours Group, later secured his involvement to speak on the multi-generational workforce to an international association of executive recruiters on whose Board I was serving, and have used him as a trusted sounding board throughout the years. His and **Discussion Partners'** research-based work highlighted in ***Executive Transitions 2 - Leveraging Experience For Future Success!*** is provocative, insightful and timeless.

**Ellie Hollander**
President and CEO, Meals on Wheels America
Former Executive Vice President and Chief People Officer, AARP


I spent my career in Human Resources before I transitioned to my next stage careers as an Advisor and member of various Boards of Directors. The advice I gave many was the same I took myself, don't retire without a plan or your decision will suffer due to the unavoidable uncertainties of your new status.  I worked closely with Tom Casey and **Discussion Partners** for several years. I benefitted from their counsel then, and monitor their progress via their blogs, books, and conversations with Tom. **DPC's** research and client experience breaks new ground as it addresses the question, "if an executive receives enterprise support to develop a post transition plan, how do they and the company mutually benefit?" **DPC's** book, *Executive Transitions 2* - provides many answers to this question.

**Greg Flores**
Founder and President, Sculpted Leaders Executive Advisory
Former Chief Human Resources Officer, TJX Companies

For many years, Tom Casey's advice and counsel has been very important to me, particularly in planning for several critical transitions during my career and retirement. The Transition Advisory services and research provided by Tom and his colleagues at **DPC** have been invaluable.

**Steve Krichmar**
Independent Trustee of Goldman Sachs Trust II Funds
Formerly Chief of Operations, Putnam Investments and Partner at PwC

Tom Casey has been a professional colleague, adviser and friend for many years. Over the past year, Tom and the work of the **Discussion Partners**, has been a guiding influence in helping me to plan for and ultimately transition into retirement. I am extraordinarily grateful for the counsel and support that I received through my relationship with Tom and **DPC**.

**Jeff Yanagi**
Former Senior Vice President of Human Resources for Pegasystems, Inc.

After a decades long career in Information Technology I transitioned to my next stage careers as an Advisor, member of various Boards of Directors, and a "gentlewomen farmer." The advice I gave many was the same I took myself, don't retire without a plan or you will be sorry! I worked closely with Tom Casey and **Discussion**

**Partners,** first as a client and later as a colleague on client engagements. I benefitted from their counsel then, now, and expect to in the future. **DPC's** research and client experience on Executive Transitions is both facts based and provocative. The information contained in the book *Executive Transitions 2 - Leveraging Experience For Future Success!* is a terrific read on the very important topic of the continuity of career trajectory.

**Ina Kamenz**
President, Frost Farms
Former Chief Information Officer, Eli Lilly


Tom has amazed me with his invaluable insights and counsel in astutely guiding the transition of our fourth-generation family business across more than two decades and three generations: from second-generation WWII veteran patriarch, to third-generation baby boomers, to current fourth-generation millennials. I attribute this to his balanced combination of international corporate and family enterprise consulting experience, his specialized military training including organizational structure and his sensitivity to family dynamics in business management. Tom deeply understands human behavior, is superb at corporate strategic and transition planning, and has always been there for us when there's a challenge!

**Michael W. Tomasso**
Chief Executive Officer
The Tomasso Group (Founded 1923)


To my surprise, I found the first year of my personal transition into the next phase of my life, far easier than I expected. While I would like to take credit, the reality is my transition took a lot of thinking, planning, and most importantly—outside expertise. I had the opportunity to work with Tom Casey as I planned my retirement and "next phase." Tom brought his experience helping many people through this transition. His thoughts, and the experience of others, helped me think differently about my approach. In the end, I think my experience with Tom is a key reason my first year has been a very positive experience.

**Jim Sappington**
President, North Point Advisory LLC
Previously EVP Global Operations, Digital and Technology, McDonald's Corporation

Transition planning is the life-blood of all successful businesses. It sustains momentum, ensures continuity, and accelerates performance. I have worked with Tom Casey for over 20 years and still marvel how adroitly he counsels businesses to adopt transition planning.

**Tobey Choate**
Chief Administrative Officer, Examity Corporation

A fulfilling life comes from making wise decisions from a well thought out transition plan effectively implemented. Also learning from one's mistakes is key to fulfillment. I have known Tom Casey for 38 years and he exemplifies, from his own experiences and actions, what successful transition planning and implementation are. Everyone should read this book.

**Ernie Glickman**
Former CEO, Harbridge House, Inc. and Human Resource Consulting Managing Partner at PricewaterhouseCoopers, LLP

As an Academic, Board Member, and Advisor I can attest to the serious concerns in the C-Suite and the boardroom with the impending retirements of Baby Boomer executives. This concern is three-fold: 1) how can an organized transition be managed, 2) how can we insure that their knowledge remains resident in the organization, and 3) how can we insure the success of their successors.

Candidly blending in advice and counsel to executives on how to plan for after they leave, is a recent enterprise undertaking. I have been impressed by the early stage work of Tom Casey and **Discussion Partners** in this area. Their research and thought leadership in the domain of Executive Transitions is persuasive. I would encourage not only individual executives, but also the companies they work for to consider the best approaches to deal with this emerging trend.

**Dr. Fred Foulkes**
Professor of Management and Organizations and Director, Human Resources, Policy Institute
Questrom School of Business, Boston University


My career was quite a ride resulting in being the Chief Executive of a global Process Improvement advisory firm. Undoubtedly the biggest benefit I had was mentoring from the earliest guru in Total Quality, Dr. Joseph Juran, who began writing on the topic in the 1940s and founded our firm when he was 75! Now as I transition from day to leadership to Board matters, I am cognizant of my desire to remain engaged embarking on new pursuits. I have worked with Tom Casey for about 10 years and have benefited from his advice on our company's and my transition. I encourage you to think like Tom asserted to me on ongoing basis, "life is a series of answering the question 'what's next?'."

**Dr. Joseph Defeo**
Chairman of the Board and former Chief Executive Officer, Juran Global Inc.
Author of ***Juran's Quality Essentials for Leaders***

# Table of Contents

# Dedications

My appreciation to all the C's in my life, nuclear and extended; to my Peruvian family, which has made me feel most welcome; and, of course, the Renners.

Of special note, my appreciation to the co-authors and editors of **Discussion Partners'** previous books.

Ada Zane Renner

Ariana Pazos Aramburu

Carolina Gallese Diaz

Claire Hebert Dow

Catherine Crane Halloran

Casey Lawlor Osborne

Edward "Tobey" Choate

Eric Seubert

Gino Piaggio Valdez

Karen Warlin

Sean Brian Casey

Timothy Donahue

Tricia Lawlor Jorden

Zohy Dakota Renner

A special call out to my parents Atty. Thomas F. Casey Sr. whose 100th birthday would have been January 2019 and Eileen MJ Devaney Casey who personified "transitions" as an artist, teacher, wife, model, mother, cartoonist, and back to teaching.

# Executive Transitions 2

Leveraging Experience For Future Success!

# Introduction
## *Note from Tom Casey*

The pace of Executives transitioning from their current full-time roles is accelerating, as Boomers are getting older, while remaining vital from both health and intellectual foundations. In our first book on **Executive Transitions, Discussion Partners** shared the findings of our first party research and findings from a then sample of approximately 100 case studies on this topic.

We are now in the position of communicating more meaningful conclusions on this topic having worked with now over 500 executives on their transitions.

**Discussion Partner's** overarching conclusion is that the perspective of, *It is Time to Retire Retirement,* is an accurate characterization and both executives and their companies would benefit from comprehensive planning on this important matter.

# Chapter 1
## Introduction

The pace of baby boomer transitions is accelerating in an already dynamic world. The last several years have been turbulent. In the US political arena, there is a contentious and acrimonious contest for a prevailing point of view as to our society's moral compass. Globally, it is the best of times and worst of times as the coexistence of healthy economies with war, disease, and terrorism have engendered debates as to how to define the nature of citizenship and degrees of societal involvement in personal lives.

As adults, we should cringe when we look at the world around us. Pre-adolescent children whose families aspire to a better life are being separated from their parents. The challenging of the validity of many of our political and social institutions has reached the point where a standard refrain is now, "I can't stand to watch the news."

While watching CNN or the BBC now requires taking Xanax in advance, there remains an additional global challenge that is underappreciated. To further complicate our world in developed and developing societies, we are essentially running out of sufficient numbers of workers to address our labor needs.

There are many contributing factors: shifting demographics, workforce aspirations, immigration policies, enterprise development of incumbents, and the question of whether the solution that technology will obviate this shortfall is, indeed, realistic.

This book is focused on sensitizing executives and the companies for which they work to these unavoidable challenges, offering points of view on problem definition and solution sets.

The important takeaways for transitioning executives are four-fold:

1. It is highly likely that your success has been derived from your ability to leverage your talents in concert with others.
2. These same talents do not disappear when one transitions.
3. The ability to leverage these already impressive attributes is your primary strength as you contemplate life's next steps.
4. There most certainly will be new challenges and interesting times.

Moreover, my hope is to sensitize executives and their enterprise leadership to the scope of the problem and a mentality that, unlike the weather, conditions can be proactively changed.

The title *Executive Transitions 2-Leveraging Experience For Future Success, the second book in our series on the this important topic* is intended to reinforce the premise that the solutions that need to be created necessitate an objective appreciation of what is, in fact, reality and avoidance of self-serving and non-fact based moving-forward tactics in handling the departure of a generation of executive leaders from the workforce.

**Thomas F. Casey Jr.**
**Boston, Massachusetts**
**March 2019**

# Chapter 2
## Executive Transitions-Today's Reality

The year 2019 is one of transition for many Boomer Executives who will be reaching 65, the customary age of retirement. This cohort, based upon **Discussion Partner Collaborative's** research and client experience, suggests that independent of this milestone age, many executives:

- Have already exited the full-time work force and are pursuing a number of activities where they have control of their calendar.

- Are approaching the date with trepidation based upon personal circumstances and have decided on a 70-or-bust mentality before leaving the full-time workforce.

- Are looking forward to retirement with ideas as to where they want to spend their time but no tactical plan.

- Are enthusiastic about their impending retirement, mostly because of the comprehensiveness of their post full-time employment planning.

Although the concept of age-related retirement is being challenged, there remains something mythical about age 65, just as when most Boomers' parents left the work force. At that time however, after the Boomers' parents got their gold watch and took a cruise, the actuarial tables said they didn't have much life left to live.

But Tony Bennett, at age 92, recently collaborated with Lady Gaga on a hit album. Clint Eastwood and Robert Redford, both in their 80s just released movies in which they starred and directed. Charley Watts of the Rolling Stones and former Beatle Ringo Starr are in their late 70s and still going strong. Paul Simon, Paul McCartney are also in their mid-70s and still touring. **In Paul Simon's case at age 76 just completing his Homeward Bound tour, ostensibly his "last."**

**Discussion Partners** launched a Transition Advisory Service in 2013 after the publication of our book *Executive Transitions-Plotting The Opportunity! that captured primarily our research on this topic* Since that time, we have worked with over 500 executives in a variety of sectors on Transition matters. This second book in our series blends continued research with "client" experience.

In working with our clients **DPC** has organized our **Transition Advisory** support to executives in four phases.

**Phase 1-Preserving The Legacy.** Taking proactive steps to insure that the efforts you undertook and the success you engendered are recalled in the most-positive terms.

In **Discussion Partners'** experience, regardless of age and psychographic profile, it is prudent to substitute the question "How will I focus my energies for the next three to five years?" vs. "What will I do with the rest of my life?" This is the principle of **Inflection Point** we utilize in our discussions with executives that have an extensive work history, often with one or two employers.

## Transition Principles

The steps below represent a baseline from which we develop tactics for executives that are departing from a continuing concern.

√ **Control the Communication Process.** Avoid relying only on the formal elements of communication. There is a need to augment this effort with an informal communication process to personalize and engage in conversations with selected managers.

√ **Confirm the Legacy.** You need to find out how you are perceived. The most effective way to do this is to have a dialogue with trusted advisors and directly ask the question, "What will you remember about me?"

√ **Networking.** Classify your internal and external networks, capturing the contact information for managers who will provide insight/access for you in the future, what we refer to as the "Nifty 50." You need to capture the information for at least 50 managers. Interact with these folks at least on a quarterly basis, recognizing that the interactions will be sustainable provided the dialogue has mutual value.

√ **Relationship Sustainability.** Subsequent to the formal announcement, the first order of business is to prepare and send an email to at least these 50 executives, internal and external, embedded with preliminary thoughts as to career focus and contact information.

√ **Accessibility.** Independent of the networking activity above, there is a need to utilize multiple vehicles—e-mails, social media, and the lost art of letter writing—to maintain contact with a broad number of executives.

**Phase 2-Ensuring Enterprise Continuity.** Making sure that care and thought are given to the preservation of momentum as manifested in the Succession Plan through constructive access, advice, and prescriptive documentation.

### Interim Period Issues-Post-Successor Selection

Be mindful there is oftentimes a rock-in-the-middle-of-the-river attitude that's to be avoided in a post-announcement environment. We usually find that this attitude is well-intentioned and focused on the executive's best interests so as to not bother them.

Still, it is difficult to work in an environment that seems to have forgotten one has a pulse.

The key here is two-fold:

1. Don't take it personally. It is the normal cycle.
2. Consider accelerating your departure from the office in favor of working remotely as soon as possible.

Regardless of timing, there is a Snagglepuss phenomenon: the appropriate time to exit stage left. The time frame is accompanied with the likely outcome of SARA, even though it was your decision to make the transition:

- **Shock**
- **Anger**
- **Rejection**
- **Acceptance**

There will be a feeling of emotional disorientation associated with departure. But remember that **Transitions** is a platform to other areas of personal and creative expression.

**Phase 3-Rejuvenation Break.** Taking a break to recharge and reflect on the next steps in your career trajectory.

The foundation for the "Commercial Sabbatical" concept **DPC** promotes derives from our research and client experience. Based upon Executive Demographics and Aspirations, it is embedded into our hypothesis that after a period of rest, successful executives want to reengage in commercial activates.

1. **Older Executives (65 plus):** Focus on two or three activities part-time post-employment.
2. **Bridge Executives (55 to 65):** Focus on two or three activities of part-time post-employment for a period of approximately two years then return to work in an advisory and/or employee capacity at a level of approximately 50% of the time until age 65 or older.
3. **Off-Ramp/On-Ramp Executives (55 and below):** If not focused on an immediate replication of a full-time setting, the executive focuses on two or three activities for approximately one year then returns to work as an advisor and/or employee until age 65 at a level in excess of 50%.

**Phase 4-Cyclical Planning.** Conceptualization, deliberation, and implementation of the plan developed prior to departure and refined subsequently.

**The most important assets a Transitioning executive has are cognizance of their abilities and readiness to leverage these skills in pursuit of new and exciting opportunities.**

# Chapter 3
## Discussion Partners Research Foundation-Executive Transitions

**Discussion Partners'** creation of our **Transition Advisory** came by accident. In 2012, we were asked to develop a "Pulse Survey" for high net worth executives over the age of 55 on the topics of Succession Strategy and Post-Retirement Planning, for a US based Association.

In order to have sufficient statistical legitimacy and to derive meaningful conclusions, at least 500 of these surveys were needed. We received over 2,000 responses.

Here are the key points of the research:

- Succession Plans, if they exist at all, assume, without executive consultation, that everyone will retire at age 65.
- But executives have a retirement range from 62 to "I don't know but no later than 65" with age 58 receiving honorable mention.

- Over 90% of the executives in our study would prefer to have a gradual phase-down in time commitment beginning at age 62 and ending at 66.
- Over 80% of the executives indicated that their companies existing Human Capital practices did not allow for a phase down.
- Over 50% of CEOs in a survey follow-up stated that they would embrace a phase-down strategy if they could keep a key executive longer while an additional 9% stated, "Not sure but should be explored."
- Over 70% of executives stipulated that the focus of their transition planning was predominantly, if not exclusively, financial.

**Research Conclusions**

Our research led us to a working hypothesis focused on ensuring that transitioning executives retained their energy and enthusiasm for their work during the period prior to retirement. This is, of course, related to the enterprise having a robust pre-departure continuity strategy.

We concluded that if the executive and the enterprise are to mutually benefit during this transition period, a dialogue must ensue that embodies the following principles:

- Succession Planning cannot be realistic unless those who are deemed inclusions (executives and those in key roles) are consulted about their contemplated retirement timing without prejudice; in other words, the timing is fluid and can be modified.

- The principle of flexibility is a must-have in Succession Planning in order to maximize, leverage and create the most options for the enterprise, executive, and potential replacements.

- Human Capital processes must allow for flexibility, as illustrated by the "phase down" concept and other options to optimize what we refer to as Human Asset Sustainability.

- Gen X and Millennial employees have stated their desire to be mentored by Boomers in order to download and carry forward the Institutional Memory; there must be a disciplined approach to facilitate this learning.

- Transition Planning support is highly desired and should be provided to key executives and those in critical roles within two years of retirement.

**DPC's** client work, which began in 2013 subsequent to the publication of our book *Executive Transitions—Plotting The Opportunity!* and now numbers over 500 clients, also suggests that retiring executives will focus on a combination of two or three of 14 part-time alternatives as exemplified in the following graph.

**Human Asset Sustainability—Plotting The Opportunity**

**A Scenario Plan exploring Transition Advice embedded with Enterprise Need:**

1. New Role/Alternative Employer
2. Consultant
3. Academic
4. Author
5. Personal Investor
6. Board Member
7. Political Involvement

8. Philanthropy
9. Social Responsibility
10. Spirituality
11. Higher Education
12. Arts
13. Start Up Initiator
14. Sports

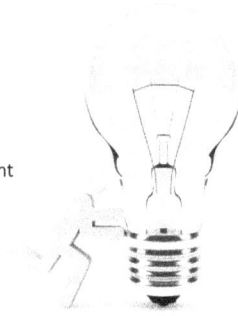

**Discussion Partners** perceives the departure of executives as a given; the new normal. What is absent is a mutually beneficial strategy that embodies the above principles.

### Retirement Planning Myths

A final set of considerations arose from **DPC's** research, supported by the work of Tammy Erickson, arguably one of the globe's thought leaders on the multi-generational workforce: There are common retirement planning myths to which many of us subscribe:

1. There is a set age when people plan to retire.
2. For the transition to be effective, organizations *require* full-time commitment from transitioning executives.
3. Executives have a well-thought out transition plan.
4. Human Capital programs currently possess the flexibility to meet the challenges of the Baby Boomer age cohort.

Our belief is that Enterprise Sustainability will be disenfranchised if planning for Executive Transitions is not an embedded strategic priority.

As executives and employers who are focused on Enterprise Growth and Differentiated Sustainability, consider the following questions:

1. How can the enterprise replenish its leadership population if its Succession Plan is based upon incorrect assumptions, such as the belief that all executives plan on staying until age 65 and/or designated successors are fully prepared?

2. How can an enterprise exploit the talents and maximize the unique perspective of the older worker, regardless of when they started their career with the company?

3. How can an executive maximize their contribution if, as they approach retirement, they are distracted by the reality that they are bereft of a comprehensive and personal non-financial transition plan?

Do you have the answers for your company? If not, you should begin a rigorous dialogue with your key executives.

There is no question that those of us in the Leadership Effectiveness domain, whether we are employers, researchers, consultants, or practitioners, need to challenge our assumptions and be more innovative if we are to influence vs. be influenced by the rapidly shifting demographics. At this point, we find it advisable to introduce the concept of the Null Hypothesis, which presumes that all of our assumptions regarding the effectiveness and efficiency of our Succession Planning protocols are incorrect! If you concur that it is time to focus attention on the presumption that our biases are incorrect, it is necessary to lay an appropriate data-driven and anecdotal-rich foundation.

# Chapter 4
## Actuarial Anxiety OR
## Why I Miss Spider-Man!

Recently, I was up at four a.m. for a flight I take frequently from Boston to JFK to meet with clients.

Those of you who fly to Kennedy on American Airlines know that once you have landed, you are assaulted by advertisements for Broadway shows, one of which is—or was—*Spider-Man*.

This ad holds special significance for me because my youngest nephew, Pierro, thinks he is Spider-Man! This perspective is reinforced constantly by his Peruvian and US family, who are shameless in buying every conceivable accessory to reinforce his image as the sticky savior of New York City.

That morning, as I was readying myself to wish Pierro a *buenos dias*, I realized the sign had been removed and replaced with a mutual fund ad with the caption, "In 1960 your life expectancy was 67. Now it is 78!"

Being 69 and being facile in simple though not complex math, I thought, "Oh !@#*, I only have nine years left!"

Not the best way for an early morning and long day to kick off!

The rudeness of the reminder of my imminent demise did, however, prompt me to spend some time on-line at the Social Security website.

The good news is that according to the website, I have until 84 and a statistical shot at 92 if I put down the cheeseburger and pick up the salad fork. I hope the Retirement Advisors are better at investing than demographics.

Please don't get me wrong. I don't reject the senior discounts at movies, but the aging process does require some adjustments in thinking.

We can't reject aging, but it's preferable to the alternative.

We can, however, reject feeling old, like a watch that is winding down slowly.

I have had the personal philosophy of looking forward, not back, with the assumption that whatever decisions I made then were well-considered, and I have already incorporated lessons I learned into how I behave.

I would rather look forward to the minutes, days, and years ahead thinking positively and enjoying the ride!

However, I do miss Spider-Man!

# Chapter 5
# Building The Bench-It Takes Years To Get It Right!

The critical first step in Executive Transitions is to insure a mutual soft landing for both the company and the executive. Unfortunately, the ability to satisfy both sets of interests requires that a plan has been in place to cope with the eventuality of the executive's departure.

**The True Test of a Succession Plan: Its Practicality and Utility Value**

As we entered 2019 and updated our resolutions, my colleagues at **Discussion Partners** and I strongly urged an elevation of, and renewed attentiveness to, **Succession and Continuity** planning as a priority to our clients.

Notwithstanding pre-existing protocols, we suggest that this review encompass the most generous interpretation of processes concomitant with experimental and disruptive solution sets.

Our recommendation is driven by the results of a recent completed study **DPC** conducted with 1,800 C-Suite participants. The survey was on the topic of envisioned enterprise challenges. Of those surveyed, 91% indicated "the ability to attract, motivate, and retain top talent" as their #1 concern.

**Discussion Partners has been conducting this annual Pulse survey since our founding in 2007. While always on the list, the intensity of the above concern was never #1 until 2018. The rationales expressed in the anecdotal justifications are compelling and include envisioned shifting demographics, new worker expectations, disruption of organization models, competitive pressures, globalization, and ineffective human capital practices.**

Our recommendation is further reinforced by a review of the recent literature on this topic.

1.  The historically low US unemployment rate
2.  The strategic imperative for Talent **depth** to be an asset rather than a liability as referenced in consolidated research on Leadership Succession/ Continuity, most recently in a series of articles in *McKinsey Insights, HBR and Sloan Management Review*
3.  The point of view that has emerged from our **2018** advisory work that **2019** represents an opportunity to use a "Disruptive Organization Model" for Talent processes overall and Leadership matters in particular

As further justification for this **recommendation,** the following foundation is provided.

-   The recently released book *Talent Wins* by Ram Charan, Dominic Barton, and Dennis Carey unreservedly states that to be competitive an organization must put "People First" while recommending the G3 process of collaboration among the CEO, CFO, and CHRO to be effective.

- Dr. Noel Tichy, in his recent book **Succession,** asserts that without proactive planning on how to fill and build an inventory of talent *well in advance* of leadership and/or key role vacancies, the chance of success is below 50% for replacement personnel.

- Ram Charan, in his book **The Attackers Advantage** and **HBR** articles, offers the following (paraphrased): *Leaders (Directors, Owners, CEO's) who excel at selection are willing to expand the lens in how they look at the capabilities of reporting levels beyond performance track record to the two or three interwoven predictive behaviors that will be necessary for success.*

- The following recent data points are from various sources (**Booz Allen, McKinsey, Boston Consulting Group, Hedrick & Struggles, Korn Ferry** and **Saratoga Institute**):

  o Team Building and Empathy are as important **as** Performance for promoting enterprise success (often stated, infrequently realized).

  o **55%** of the *Fortune* 500 Boards of Directors have expressed dissatisfaction with the Succession Planning processes of their enterprises, including the CEO replacement approach.

  o A study of the **2500** largest companies on the planet indicate that inefficient **Succession Planning** results, on average, in $1.8-billion losses during transition.

  o **39%** of the *Fortune* 1000 Boards indicate "no viable candidate" to replace the CEO, compelling a similar percent of external hires that Charan stipulates as "highly unlikely to be successful."

**DPC's** conclusion that Succession Planning takes years, not months, leads us to recommend the following steps:

1. Senior level stakeholder interviews focused on beyond-task proficiency. What are the essential differentiating qualities that will be needed for success?
2. Comparative Inventory of Leaders (broad based) and high potentials in relationship to these attributes
3. Embed into developmental and hiring strategies the lessons learned from this exercise.
4. Creation of a **Critical Constituency Depth Chart** whereby the following is highlighted:
   a. Identification of one ready-now replacement
   b. Identification of two possible replacements
   c. Identification of external Search capabilities to be deployed in emergencies and/or lack of a ready-now sense of urgency
   d. Assignment of non-senior leaders in a personal growth and development task similar to the **GE** "popcorn stand" to provide additional evaluative foundation

The **New England Patriots** have a mantra of "do your job," promoted by Coach Bill Belichick. Their **six** Super Bowl wins indicates the validity of this philosophy. **DPC's** above suggestions represent process steps that should be **presently underway**. If they aren't, a **sense of urgency** should exist. **DPC** would substitute Belichick's words with "do the job you should have been doing all along!"

Additionally, we would embed the following questions:

I. **What skills sets will we need beyond domain proficiency to have a sustainable growth—oriented enterprise?**

II.  How does our current population of Leaders and Future Leaders compare to these desired attributes?

III.  How can we develop and/or hire sufficient numbers of people to address deficiencies in the above?

IV.  What is the true nature of our Leadership bench in respect to Readiness?

V.  What is our contingency plan to be deployed if necessary?

From whatever vantage point you occupy, the next several years will be dynamic. As a suggestion, borrowing a title from a previous book by Dr. Tichy on the topic of Succession: *Control Your Destiny Or Somebody Else Will!*

# Chapter 6
## The Lack of Success In Succession Planning

Recent editions of the *Harvard Business Review* were devoted to talent-related issues such as Collaboration and Feedback. This is not unusual. What is provocative is that talent is NOW a separate and distinct strategic intent rather than a subordinate process as manifested by the importance it is being given in the business press.

**CNN, CNBC** and **Bloomberg** are now airing Public Service Announcements with the President of **SHRM,** the Society for Human Resources Management, who is speaking on the topics of the current reality of the labor shortage and its implications for achieving strategic intents.

Several data points contained in these articles and PSAs refer to CEO Succession status consistent with previously mentioned **DPC** client experience:

- The median tenure of a *Fortune 500* CEO is now less than five years.
- Over 50% of *Fortune 500* Board Members are dissatisfied with their company's Succession Planning process.

- Succession Planning is an insular process that usually achieves a level of seriousness approximately 18 months before transition.
- The rules are being broken with respect to the age of Board Members today. In 1987, only 3% were age 60; now over 30% are 65 or above, which reflects both the shifting demographics and enterprise desire for optimization of executive wisdom.

The above focuses on CEOs. One can speculate without likelihood of contradiction that the process is even more deficient below the level of CEO.

A terrific client once called us and said, "Can you come to Florida? I think I have a problem."

This executive had recently assumed the role of Director of Strategy for a very large organization, and during onboarding, had reviewed the organization's Succession Plan. He was struck by the assumption, as was I when I reviewed the oppressively large document, that every key executive (and/or those in critical roles) was planning on retiring at 65!

The good news was that the enterprise had an approach. This was unusual as research indicates that only about 36% of companies actually create a Succession Plan.

The bad news was that the Succession Plan was mathematically driven not only by the anticipated retirement age but also the determination of readiness based upon Performance and Competency scores.

This awareness led us to ask an important question: Has anyone asked the executives about their retirement plans?

The answer was, "No, not as part of this process." What?

My colleagues and I were asked to do some interviews with key executives and incumbents in essential positions, and we learned the following:

- The retirement age of 65 was arbitrary. Some folks were planning on leaving sooner, some later based on circumstances.

- The executives and incumbents were reluctant to be specific as to retirement age because a) they did not want to be a lame duck and/or b) they did not want to be locked in to an age or date.

- The organization's ideas regarding position replenishment were filled with words such as "Maybe this person," "I think they are the most likely," or, most frequently, "We will have to go outside to find the replacement."

- All executives were open to phasing down over a period of years and extending their tenure with the organization in their current or an alternative capacity.

- Most had a financial plan yet seemed to be a little vague on the details.

- Few had a clear idea as to their life plan beyond a) playing golf; b) spending time with the family; c) sitting on Boards; d) traveling; e) getting involved with churches or charities.

- Most felt unprepared and desirous of the enterprise to assist more in the Post-Employment Planning aspect of the transition.

Our conclusion with this company, and later with other clients, was that although there was a plan, its usefulness as an accurate characterization of options and opportunities was suspect.

There were additional observations from the above client that were borne out in subsequent assignments with other companies:

1. Life-planning resources are somewhat limited as they are often offered as an employee benefit rather than integrated with the enterprise's Succession Plan.

2. For the most part, vendor services are outplacement methodologies reverse-engineered for potential retirees. Although not a condemnation of these approaches, our research found that the more seasoned or specialized the executive, the more they felt the effort to plan for transition was an attempt to put them out to pasture and, in some cases, was premature.

3. The other modality of Life Coach, borrowing from the Army, is "be all you can be." Or back in the 1980s, "What color is my parachute?" When it comes to executive sentiment, there is more concern about the parachute opening than its color.

4. Executives want to plan their after-work life like they would their business endeavors, with options, risk assessments, tactics, and success metrics.

## Augmentation of Lessons Learned

Since the launch of **DPC's** Transition Advisory practice, we have derived the following principles reinforced by the research of Tammy Erickson and Bob Morison in their *HBR* article, "It is Time to Retire Retirement":

- Succession Planning cannot be realistic unless those who are deemed inclusions (executives and those in key roles) play a role in their contemplated retirement timing and appropriate transition steps.
- A foundational element for executives is the efficacy of their financial planning. Has sufficiency been ascertained?
- Transition planning support is highly desired and appreciated by this constituency provided the service is delivered well in advance of retirement and executed in business terms.
- The principle of flexibility is a must-have in Succession Planning in order to maximize leverage and create the most options for the enterprise, executive, and potential replacements.

The biggest obstacle we have found is the reluctance of the enterprise to redefine work to embed flexibility. The strongest example is the willingness of executives to incorporate a gradual phase-down into career-stage management, yet our research indicated that only 50% of CEOs are willing to discuss this approach; this number is likely to go up as the recession recedes. The problem is they have not been educated about the implications of the shifting demographics nor have they been asked to provide input as to possible solutions such as phase down.

One case in point is a CFO where a) the succession plan had her leaving at 65 with no ready-now replacement on the depth chart; b) the incumbent's *unexpressed* desire was to leave at 63, BUT; c) she would be willing to stay until 67 provided she could phase down to 50% of work time during the four year period between ages 63 and 67.

In this case, we were told by HR that the CEO and Board would never agree to a phase down, yet when we met with the CEO and noted that with a phase down, the company would have the services of the CFO for an additional four years *and* have a more likely successor, he was all for it.

Given that the fastest growing segment of the domestic workforce is over the age of 55 (see Exhibit 1 below), it is incumbent upon all of us to challenge our assumptions regarding the nature of work to be done, the time spent doing it and who is doing the work.

Our position is that without this point of view, Succession Plans will simply be more a fiction than a powerful leadership effectiveness tool.

The principle of "Retiring Retirement," as espoused by Erickson and Morison, has to be a key workforce planning strategy.

**Exhibit 1**

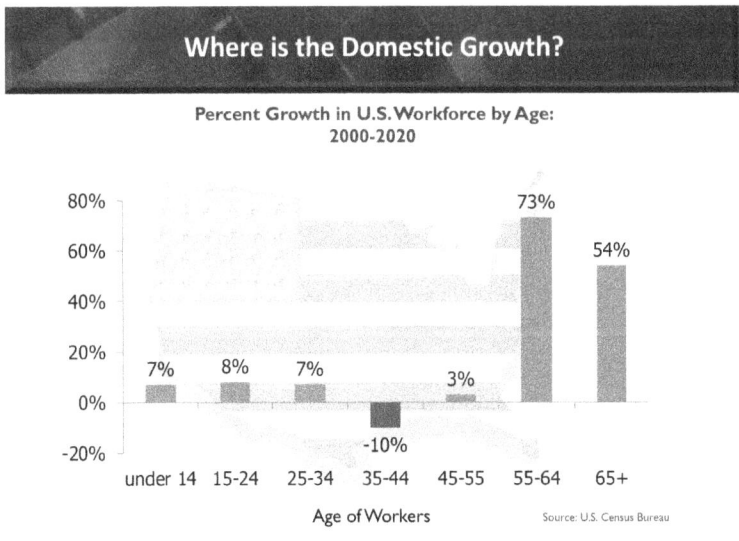

# Chapter 7
## Succession Planning Risks-Tenure Without Age!

As Baby Boomers ponder retirement, there is the inevitable question, "What do I do next?" **A huge risk for enterprise Succession Plans is that Generation X executives of longer tenure are likely to be asking the same question.**

A CNBC segment once referred to retirement planning as the "no-huddle offense." Essentially, there is a need to accelerate not only the economic preparation for retirement but also the determinants as to how one will spend their time for Boomers and where will I spend it for Generation X …

Tammy Erickson's multiple books on shifting demographics, particularly, **What's Next Gen X?** and Dr. Lynda Gratton's recent book **The 100 Year Life** forcefully remind us that traditional perspectives regarding retirement *and career management* are outmoded.

The need to reflect and plan is now being down-aged (late 40s to early 50s) to encompass long-serving incumbents that began working with their present employers at an early age.

Put yourself in the position of one of these incumbents. This is their thought process:

- I started with this company right out of school.
- I am 48 years old.
- I like the company. It has been good to me.
- I like my role and feel I am making a contribution, BUT!!!
- I wonder what it would be like to work somewhere else, AND!!!!
- I need to decide now before it is too late.

For those of us in our 60s, 48 is young. However, I assert that none of us felt that way when we were 48!

The inherent problems with the above reflections are: a) the employee may leave a good situation just for the sake of leaving; and b) the company is at risk of a brain drain at the nexus point of identification of future leaders and sustainability.

Engagement surveys, while informative, do not drill down sufficiently beyond the question, "Are you happy now?" In addition, those that are struggling with this dilemma are most likely reflecting on it privately and not sharing it with the organization.

While researching our 2015 book **Inflection Points-Risk Readiness Failure Fearless** on career decision points, Sean Casey, Adriana Pazos Aramburu and I became of aware this phenomenon.

**DPC** perceived the issue to be a serious risk to our client population that has longer- serving employees. Consequently, using the mantra "it is better to be supportive than short-sighted," we have been piloting a Coaching interdiction with several companies that fit the above profile.

Trajectory Advisory Service focuses on asking and answering the question for those who are in their late 40s and have approximately 15 years enterprise tenure: "Is this company and role sufficiently challenging and engaging for you to want to stay?"

**DPC** began piloting this offering in mid-2016 and has worked with 90 clients. Our findings are tenfold based upon the admittedly modest sample:

1.  100% of those with whom we worked admitted to having given "serious thought" to making a change.
2.  100% of those with whom we worked, although initially skeptical, appreciated the proactivity of their company in providing resources to assist in their decision making.
3.  90+% were applying loose criteria to their thought process and were focused more on "now" vs. "where or why."
4.  Approximately the same % felt the restraint on making an informed decision was due more to "what if I don't like it" vs. the transition being a sensible career move.
5.  Eighty-one of the 90 clients decided to stay with their present employer.
6.  **DPC** worked with nine clients on a soft landing in which the company was able to secure a replacement in advance of separation and the departing member was supported in their search (search firms, references, time to interview etc.).
7.  Each of the 81 clients that chose to remain was provided with an enterprise-supported **Engagement Driver** as a safety valve to reinforce the prudence of their decision making.
8.  The range of "Drivers" encompassed new roles, new locations, NGO participation, Commercial Board sponsorship, paid sabbatical, education, reconfigured work hours and innovative solutions.

9.  None of the 81 clients received additional nor special compensation for what I would invoke as the obvious reasons.

The #10 Finding from the Pilot is that **65%** of those with whom **DPC** worked indicated they would have left in large part due to curiosity and feelings of intellectual stagnation.

The overarching conclusion **DPC** derived from this effort is that organizations that have the above profile are best served by being proactive, supportive, and sincere in working with their incumbents. If they don't, they run the risk of being controlled by vs. controlling their Talent Readiness posture due to unanticipated and undesired departures.

# Chapter 8
## Nostalgia Of Selective Memory

About a year ago, my son was in the hospital for a long time. He is an active adult with two young boys, and he was, as he put it, "bored to tears."

I visited him one Saturday and listened to him complain that there was nothing to watch on TV. Sympathetic parent that I am, and also having been laid up for an extended period in my 20s, I barked, "Stop your whining. At least you have cable!"

For fellow Boomers, I can imagine you are also harkening back to when you were told by your parents, "I had to walk five miles to school in a blizzard."

Growing up in the 1960s was not always easy, but it was memorable. Looking back, we can now compare how some of our rites of passage and the things we did were striking in their differences to today's rites of passage and how things are done.

One difference is the use of sunscreen. Back then, Coppertone was a luxury for many. Most of us burned, peeled, burned, and peeled again until Labor Day.

Seat belts were available but usually ignored. I was the oldest of seven children. Once at a party, I spoke to the youngest of nine, and we reminisced that on short drives in convertibles, she was positioned above the back seat while her older brothers held her legs. Today, this would be considered reckless and dangerous. Back then, parents had a lot of kids but only one car.

Transistor radios were the form of non-visual news and entertainment. They required a battery. Batteries became even more necessary during a power outage. As the oldest, I was once asked to go out and buy a battery during the early stages of a hurricane. When my mother questioned the wisdom of this, my father said, "You have to think long term. If he blows away, it's one less college tuition." My mother's response was, "Good luck, honey."

You can see the origin of my parental sympathy gene!

Halloween was a great time. We sometimes went to the best candy provider three times without changing costumes. I don't recall my parents having to be human X-ray machines to make sure we were going to be safe while gorging on our bounty. Jimmy Kimmel would have no post-Halloween "I ate your candy" segments as our candy hoard rarely survived until the next day.

We didn't think of candy as junk food. It was an annual entitlement.

I have no appreciation of how many TV options we have now. When I was growing up, we only had three, all ending in C. For the longest time, if you had a color TV, you could only watch two shows: *Bonanza* and *Disney*. The national news was only 30 minutes a night (this is probably the aspect of growing up I miss the most!).

Well, in truth, I probably miss the one-speed bike the most. Today's transport modes are too confusing!

The pace of innovation is increasing, and memories are getting shorter. I vividly recall my 10-year-old grandson spying a flip phone and asking, "What's that?" I shudder to think of him being exposed to a rotary dial!

I don't recall feeling I had it easy when I was growing up. Just the opposite.

I do reflect now, as a parent and grandparent, that it certainly was different. Not better nor worse. Just memorable.

# Chapter 9
# Protecting Legacy-The Concept of The Playbook

**Discussion Partners** perceives the first order of business of an about-to-depart executive as focusing not only on enterprise continuity but also on preserving their legacy.

In our work with executives, we actively encourage the development of a leave-behind document we refer to as **The Playbook.**

This suggestion may seem odd, but our experience is that **The Playbook** is very useful when an identified Successor may not be up to the task initially.

The development of **The Playbook** is also non-trivial reaffirmation of legacy, as transparency is always appreciated and oftentimes goes unchallenged.

The value of creating a brief treatise on your experience is it a) helps others see your role through your eyes and b) reduces blowback in that after you leave, it reduces the possibility that you will be blamed for others' mistakes.

Our concept is a two- or three-page memorandum that focuses on the following:

- The initiatives you feel were executed well
- Those that are in process and/or you feel were deficient
- Two or three top-of-the-mind suggestions for securing progress in your previous role

In the 1980s, several artists got together to record the song *We Are the World* in support of famine relief. Quincy Jones, the producer, posted a sign for the artists to see as they entered the studio: **Leave Your Egos At The Door.** Unfortunately, although all of the artists appeared in a picture taken before the recording session, there was no post-recording group photo because there had been ego defections during the project.

The concept of **The Playbook**, beyond transparency and information, is decency. Make sure that everyone benefits from your insights.

When embedding the above recommendation, we were influenced heavily by President George H.W. Bush's traditional "President's Letter," the document left for those assuming the office. He was being replaced by Bill Clinton, who had beaten him in the election.

Focused on providing support for his successor, his closing comments in the letter were, "You will be OUR President when you read this note."

Ego and history aside, the seriousness of this type of memorandum is a terrific asset for the departing executive's reputation and for the incomer's insight.

# Chapter 10
## Edgy While Being Absent

A major question that arises during the Succession planning process is how to manage a graceful exit when a Successor has been named and is on-site.

**Pre-Departure Dislocation**

**DPC** has found that many executives feel awkward or uncomfortable while continuing with their employer when their Successor has been identified and on-boarded.

This discomfort is exacerbated by the fact that the executive is likely more focused on life's next chapter. **DPC** refers to this feeling of disequilibrium as "Elvis has left the building" emotion.

In these circumstances, we suggest a modality we refer to as the **3 D's Framework** as presented below:

- **Disappearance**—The executive should have significantly reduced visibility on-site unless required (counterintuitive when one is still employed, although this approach has merit).

- **Directive**—It is hard to abruptly avoid behaving like the boss. **DPC** strongly suggests that a "have you considered" rather than a "you should" approach is preferable when interacting with a Successor or key incumbents.

- **Distance**—To support the Succession plan, it is preferable to avoid being the wizard behind the curtain but, rather, maintain a respectful distance, both logistical and relationship-wise, during the bridge tenure *with clear boundaries worked out in advance with your Successor.*

## Post-Transition Common Denominators

Regardless of age, enterprise tenure, or post-departure endeavors, **DPC** has found that there are three common denominators that, if kept at the front of the mind, contribute to success.

We have labeled the top three for *Next Generation Engagement* as follows:

1. **Edgy**—the ability to engage in activities that challenge intellectual curiosity via continued acquisition of knowledge and adjunct expertise
2. **Control**—the ability to have as much total control as possible over your calendar and the focus of your activities
3. **Relevance**—the ability to continue to promote your personal brand and be recognized as a domain expert regardless of your future setting

Many executives can't wait to get started on the next phase of life while others are somewhat fearful.

The more organized the executive is in pre-departure thinking and awareness of possible outcomes, the more likely it is that they will be comfortable with what's next!

# Chapter 11
## The Commercial Sabbatical

Age 65 is no longer the inflection point whereby we retire, get a watch, take a cruise, play some golf, and periodically look out the window to see if the Grim Reaper has found our address.

As previously noted, the increase in life expectancy and an active lifestyle are prompting Boomer executives to more seriously consider what they'll do with their post-retirement time.

In working with many executives and providing Transition Advisory Coaching in advance of retirement, one of the first lessons **DPC** learned is that the word "retirement" is outdated.

In their 2002 McKinsey Award-winning *Harvard Business Review* article "It Is Time to Retire Retirement," Tammy Erickson and Bob Morrison predicted that the traditional views on retirement were fast becoming obsolete. Their prediction in that article and later writings is *now* a reality.

Based upon **DPC's** client experience, we have observed an emerging mental model executives employ in determining how they will spend their time after a three-to-six-month period of disengagement not limited to hobbies, family time, or travel.

Alternatively, our Boomer executive clientele wants to stay engaged in commercial activities not for economic reasons but to remain, as one client put it, "relevant."

Within **DPC**, we refer to this time it takes for an executive to depart their employer and return to the workforce in some capacity as a *Commercial Sabbatical.*

Our client experience suggests that beyond Board membership, Boomer executives will return to the workforce in a part- or full-time capacity within 12 months if they retire between the ages of 58 and 62 and 18 months if they are above age 62 when they take a break.

The concept of the ***Commercial Sabbatical*** is the most-compelling finding from the Transition Advisory work of **DPC**. When our coaches are speaking to executives, helping them understand that it is only a matter of time before you are reengaged frames key elements of the planning process and confronts head-on the conscious or subconscious concern of executives regarding relevance.

**DPC** strongly recommends a rejuvenation break to clear one's head and decompress for a period of no less than three months, during which of critical importance is the need to ensure that one's networks do not go dark. This can be done via selective communication during the break and by reconnecting when the sabbatical is over.

# Chapter 12
## The Boomers' Wish List!

Age 60 is where most Boomers are at a crossroads: looking backward and forward at the same time. It's the nexus of "what did I do" with "now what?"

There are, however, a number of things on which this age cohort almost unanimously agrees:

- They wish they could walk from the car to the plane without unpacking and having to take off their shoes.
- They wish that when they get a haircut, they could refer to the person as a barber rather than as a stylist. (They would miss the massages, though!)
- They wish they were still ignorant of the dangers of the sun.
- They wish cheeseburgers with fries were classified as health food.
- They wish people hugged in the morning rather than tapping their iPhones.
- They wish other drivers would stop beeping their horns at them…and apparently no one else.

- They wish that when sitting on a plane, they did not have to deflect the back packs heading towards their faces (guns and knives are not the only things that should be considered lethal weapons).
- They wish that when they smiled, people didn't ask them what's wrong.
- They wish black and brown could be worn together.
- They wish people didn't say "huh" when they mention leisure suits.
- They wish remote controls were less complex.
- They wish there were only three networks so they didn't have to worry about what Is showing on the other 97.
- They wish hair follicles were as resistant as body fat.
- They wish their grandchildren didn't ask "What's that" when they use a flip phone.
- They wish descriptions of draft beers used clearer words.
- They wish senior citizen discounts started at 55 so they would have had more time to enjoy them.
- They wish they knew at 35 what they think they know at 60!

It is said that 60 Is the new 50, so I guess they have many more years to reflect on how we should refine our wish lists.

On my next birthday I turn 70. I prefer to also refer to it as the new 50!

# Chapter 13
## Post-Transition Aspirations of Boomer Executives

Where will executives likely spend their time post-employment? It is hard to say as among our clients we now have a Congressional candidate, the head of one of the US's largest philanthropic organizations, a touring rock star, and seven novels being written.

The most-recent research conducted by **DPC**, supported by Transition Advisory client work, concludes that post-employment Executives will continue to focus their time on 14 areas of involvement, as mentioned earlier.

We will spare you the exact words to express the sentiments, however, it should be noted that *to a person*, the **DPC** clients have indicated, "I am going to take time off before I even think about it!" And they were unanimous in their desire to avoid having to be tethered to their Smartphones, so in the first three to six months, they can be expected to drop off the grid. More on the wisdom of this later.

**14 Areas of Post-Employment Involvement**

As you peruse the list of 14 areas of involvement, PLEASE keep in mind that the most likely strategy will be a portfolio of two or three initiatives, each with a part-time commitment focus. The Executive will rebalance their portfolio on a regular basis in three areas:

### *Commercial Catalyst*

- *New Role to Alternative Employer*—This is most likely an interim managerial slot for a predetermined period of time. A *Harvard Business Review* article, "The Rise of the Supertemp," provides an excellent foundation for appreciating this strategy.

- *Consultant*—This role would be to act as external advisor on a project basis either through affiliation with a firm and/or at the request of those in the Executives network.

- *Entrepreneur*—A number of Executives want to experience a creative process by starting a venture either aligned with previous career interests or entirely different.

- *Board Member*—This is the most popular pursuit, however, it is also the one in which those Executives not already on Boards acknowledge they need a sensible strategy to get out there to be in demand.

- *Personal Investor*—These Executives want to be Angel Investors in start-up companies where they would also provide expertise and take a proactive role in governance.

- *Start Up Initiator*—This is differentiated from Angel Investor and/or Entrepreneur in that they want to transform into a role that is more like a Venture Capitalist.

### Intellectual Pursuits and Physical Fitness

- *Academics*—Most likely as an adjunct faculty member, however, a number of our clients do plan on accepting emeritus positions.

- *Author*—A number of clients have ideas for articles, books, white papers, and blogs. To a person, however, they appear to want to focus on the future of issues and/or present their thoughts on trends in their domain.

- *Higher Education*—Some executives want to complete suspended academic pursuits or remain edgy by attending executive programs.

- *Arts*—One surprising finding from **DPC's** Advisory work is the number of executives who had truncated their artistic abilities in music, theater, interior design, or artistic expression and now want to revisit these pursuits. A case in point is the client who wanted to be a rock star and is now doing session work in Tennessee and touring during the summer *while still working.*

- *Sports*—A common refrain we hear from Executives is the need to get back in shape. Their focus is to intensify the time they have left and focus on their exercise regimen.

### Community Involvement

- *Political Involvement*—For the most part, executives say their political aspirations have been channeled into fundraising and superficial domain-related advice while acknowledging they would make terrible candidates. Where they do want to get in the game, it is either in pursuit of local or statewide office or, in one case, national office.

- **Philanthropy**—Many executives manifest a desire to subsidize and or raise money for worthy NGOs in the area of personal experience or interest.

- **Social Responsibility**—Executives have the most generous interpretation of this area inclusive of a) volunteerism; b) advisory; c) governance or, in many cases, creating an NGO that focuses on a personal area of interest.

## Case in Point—Assessing One's Legacy

In Transition advisory, **DPC** works with executives on reinforcing their legacy. In the creation of this statement of reputation, we ask that they consult others regarding their insights to see if those with whom they have been associated share their self-image.

This prompts statements such as "Tim was a great staff developer" or "Paul was the best relationship manager ever."

Our client executives take justifiable pride in these accolades. They have worked hard during their careers and have focused energy to deserve such compliments.

However, the evolving nature of retirement suggests that there is a Round Two for generating a new reputation. In retirement, many executives ponder what that will be.

In our discussions with executives regarding the next phase of their careers (and we use this word purposely), the reputation statement will be less about leadership skills. It will be derived from channeling a passion into a mastery.

In our client work, we have learned a lot about passion. We describe it as "an interest in a pursuit which, for the most part, has been unfulfilled based upon enterprise role requirements."

For example, our clients have mentioned as their passions teaching at the graduate level, creating an NGO focused on children's issues, entering politics as a candidate, or becoming a studio musician.

The challenge many executives have is that it is difficult to get started on Round Two.

Our client work suggests three phases needed to turn an idea into an action:

1. Frame the pursuit of a passion in a framework similar to a business plan (Goals, Investments, Metrics, etc.).
2. Dedicate to Educate. Learn as much as possible about the experience of others who have pursued this interest.
3. Just Do It! Although this is an overused term, there is merit in recognizing that part of pursuing a passion is the willingness to accept risk.

**One conclusion we have drawn is that the likelihood of failure is very low. These former executives are more likely to be having so much fun that failure will be a non-issue!**

# Chapter 14
# I Thought I Was Old Enough To Know Myself

This chapter contains an interview with a former Congressman, now in his 70s, who in his late 40s realized that his self-perception of how he tolerated being challenged was wrong.

To set the tone for the importance of this interview with the now retired Boomer, we need to appreciate that this has been a difficult period for tolerance in the United States. Part of our political landscape is anti-immigration to the point where building a wall across the US's southern border is considered worth a government shutdown.

As a society, we are still reeling from the Charleston shooting and Charlottesville white supremacist march, the reactions to which have aggravated racial tension in the US.

Police reactions to racial relations are strained and satirized by comedians venturing, "The only way to avoid being shot is a) don't wear a hoodie; b) don't be big…and don't be black." Somehow, we think this is funny!

It is easy to be cynical when we hear the words "black lives matter" and respond "all lives matter." Yet our reality is much different. The progress of the #MeToo Movement does not appear to have made much of a difference in racial relations.

Years ago, there was a TV series called *L.A. Law*. In one episode, defense lawyers ask a judge to recuse himself from the trial of a black defendant by presenting him with statistical evidence that his decisions and sentences are blatantly racist.

If presented with such evidence, one would expect the character (or, in real life, someone who feels they are open-minded) to be defensive.

In this episode, the judge does the right thing and recuses himself. He is self-aware enough to know he is not self-aware.

We are all intolerant to a degree. This trait is not part of our DNA but a learned behavior. The questions before any individual who thinks of himself as tolerant are: a) how do you know if your self-image of tolerance is delusional; and b) what do you do if faced with your subconscious intolerance?

We were fortunate to find an executive who was willing to share his experiences. What is of particular interest is that this executive was known as an advocate for tolerance on all levels when he was in Congress.

### Executive Interview-Former Congressman

*During my formative years, I was privileged. Consequently, my personal philosophy and points of view about race relations, immigration and other issues were based on reading, discussions, not experience.*

*I always thought of myself as tolerant regarding people who were different, whether it was race, political orientation, sexual preference, etc.*

*Unfortunately, I was wrong.*

*I was giving a speech out of state and got lost on the way back to the airport. This was in the days before iPhones. Lost meant lost. I had an associate with me who was driving the rental car.*

*We wandered into a distressed neighborhood and stopped to get our bearings. I noticed three young men of color not far away who were clearly aware of our presence. We were unsettled. They started walking toward us, and in an attempt to drive away, we crashed the car.*

*They kept coming, actually now running. When they got to us, they said, "Are you guys ok? Do you need some help?" They could not have been nicer. They got us to the airport, arranged for a rental car company. They were great.*

*Flying back home, I could not help thinking about how scared I was and why. Clearly it was the neighborhood, the circumstances, and, more importantly, the three young men being black.*

*I asked myself this question: Even in a rough neighborhood, if they were white, dressed in khakis wearing Izod shirts, would I have reacted the same way?*

*Clearly not.*

*What also got my attention was when I relayed what happened to others. Their response was disheartening as they commented, "I would have been scared, too." Also, "You got lucky."*

*When I look back on that event, I realize that even with a narrow definition of the word, I am a racist. It shook my self-image, and now I try to be mindful of who I am, not who I thought I was.*

*The question before me at that time and now is to channel this awareness, minimizing the damage it can cause, and maybe even using the awareness to do some good.*

The openness of the Congressman was refreshing. His candor forces us to ask these questions:

- We are all intolerant of some things or many things, but how do we address challenges to our self-image when confronted?
- When we are confronted with our true beliefs or tendencies, we can behave in one of two ways: ignore it or attempt to channel it in appropriate ways. But how do we respond?

**Self-awareness is an asset; self-respect an aspiration; self-direction, in a positive way, an obligation even when it challenges who you really are as a person.**

# Chapter 15
## The Importance of Networking

A well-known fact in the consulting sector is that career longevity is derived from two factors: a super-pleasing engagement driving customer satisfaction and ongoing maintenance of networks.

A former colleague told the story of the importance of maintaining networks as it led to his recent marriage. In 1995 while on an expat assignment, he had a client with whom he had maintained only electronic contact for over a dozen years. Admittedly she was on his C list, but she would hear from him every five or six months via e-mail. This e-contact consisted of no more than "how is it going" or "you may be interested in this" tidbits prompting one word responses of "Fine" or "Thanks."

However, he had occasion to visit the country of his former assignment, prompting more-robust conversation with this client, and now they are married. This prompts the question, "What if, when the client engagement ended, so did the relationship?"

We are not attempting to submit a script for the Lifetime Channel but rather are attempting to make a commercial point: *Relationships matter.*

More specifically, **DPC's** work with pre-retirement executives has compelled us to reinforce the point: *Never be forgotten even after you go!*

We use as reinforcement a story once told by John Wayne (yes, we are that old) about the career phases of an actor's appeal to directors.

1. "Who is John Wayne?"
2. "Get me John Wayne!"
3. "How long can John Wayne be John Wayne?"
4. "Get me someone like a younger John Wayne!"
5. "Who was John Wayne?"

There are some unassailable truths emerging from our work with **DPC's** executives as they plan their retirements. Here are some of them:

- They will endeavor to remain/get re-involved in commercial activity within a reasonable period post-retirement.
- We perceive retirement to be a series of "on ramps and off ramps," as postulated by Tammy Erickson and Bob Morison in their book *Workforce Crisis*.
- The most expeditious way to re-engage in commercial activities is to never disconnect from important networks.
- Staying connected takes time and thoughtful planning. The other party has to see the benefit intrinsic to the relationship or it will go dark.

We strongly think that it is not advisable to be referred to by a director as "Who was John Wayne?"

In the strongest possible terms, we advise executives to focus considerable energy on relationship cultivation at all junctures of their career to maintain the flexibility to access the "on ramp" at any time.

The importance of networking also underscores the importance of building and managing your digital brand. Currently, without question, LinkedIn is the most-commonly accepted professional networking tool, so executives must learn how to leverage it. Remember, LinkedIn and other executive networking sites are not about your first connections but rather the power and clout of your second connections. As part of Transition Planning, the executive needs to methodically migrate both their active and dormant relationships into LinkedIn. With a plethora of LinkedIn tool extensions, you can productively manage your network to pursue particular opportunities or just keep your network current and vibrant.

# Chapter 16
## Remember The Alamo

I have some friends who were visiting San Antonio on a business trip. They decided to see the local sights, such as River Walk, and, of course, The Alamo.

San Antonio can be very hot in September, and such was the case that day.

A number of tourists were waiting to enter, including a mother with her child, Jennifer.

**Executive Narrative**

*Jennifer was hot, cranky, and uncooperative as her mother beseeched her to "stay in the shade." She practiced the art of "No, I don't have to."*

*Those of you who have visited the Alamo know the security officers dress like olden Texas Rangers, complete with the boots, six-shooter belt, and, of course, the big Stetson!*

*The mother, in frustration, said within hearing of Jennifer, "Officer, can you help me get my daughter to behave?"*

*Jennifer was paying close attention as the officer tipped his hat, said, "Yes, ma'am," hoisted his belt, and began ambling towards our little princess.*

*Jennifer broke the land speed record racing to her mother saying, "I'm sorry, Mommy"!*

**Executive Insights**

**The wisdom of age is the major benefit of getting older. So is the ability to activate Networks!**

# Chapter 17
## Board or Bored

As Baby Boomers contemplate retirement or post full-time employment, the inevitable question arises, "What do I do next?"

Essentially, there is a need to accelerate not only the economic preparation for retirement but also the determinants as to how one will spend their time.

Tammy Erickson's and Lynda Gratton's books on shifting demographics forcefully remind us that traditional perspectives regarding retirement are outmoded. In fact, Boomers are likely to remain active by engaging in multiple activities.

A recent Pulse Survey of over 1,000 executives conducted by **DPC** posed two questions: "How far evolved are your retirement plans?" and "How will you spend your retirement time?"

The responses regarding preparation caused concern for the executives as they indicated that while they had spent some time "thinking" about retirement, there was an absence of planning.

The top four answers on time commitment were:

1. Generate income through part-time employment
2. Spend time with the family
3. Focus on physical well-being,
4. Seek Board opportunities

While the respondents could explain their retirement goals in general terms, they had little disciplined thinking about how to achieve them. This was particularly true regarding affiliation as a Board member. The survey participants, while clear on what they could offer as a Board member, were less clear as to how to go about securing positions.

The good news is that Boards value the talents of Boomers. As an example, *Harvard Business Review* suggests that rules are being broken with respect to the age of Board members. In 1987, only 3% were age 60; now 35% are 65 or older, which is indicative of both the shifting demographics and enterprise desire for the preservation of institutional memory.

However, for those who have never been a Board member, getting a position on a Board is not analogous to a Field of Dreams: "If they know I am available, they will come!"

Based upon our experience, we recommend the following steps for those who want to pursue both non-governmental organizations (NGOs) and/or Commercial Board opportunities:

- Positive networking with **all** in your network
- Establishing relationships with entities whose Board needs match the aspirant's capabilities
- Exploring Social Networking sites on NGOs with the assumption that a need exists for advisory support

- Disciplined interaction with the Executive Search consultants with whom you had pre-retirement contact

## Visibility Through Social Media

Leverage your interest in Board Memberships using vehicles such as LinkedIn. We strongly take the view that opportunities are unlikely to be local. With the commonplace acceptance of remote work styles supported by robust and less-expensive digital tools, executives are increasingly designing a portfolio of activities that is geographically dispersed. Essentially, constructing the right post-employment portfolio can trump the geographical proximity of opportunities. Geographical independence afforded to the post-employment executive exponentially enlarges the number and diversity of opportunities and requires thoughtful transition planning. This strategy is essential for Board of Director aspirations.

## A Cautionary Note

**Board Memberships**-As this is a likely area of pursuit, we wanted to provide some additional detail. **DPC** has a matrix approach to thinking of Board positions based upon membership, committees, and leadership. Our conclusion has been regardless of which slot or slots the executive fills, they should be on no more than three Boards, thus avoiding becoming a professional member and unintentionally working close to full time.

# Chapter 18
## The Celebration Without The Party!

Ask yourself this question: "What if I invited my family to my birthday party and no one came?"

Your obvious feelings would be confusion, rejection, hurt, and if a member of my family, a vow of "I'll make them pay"!

Now ask yourself the question, "What if I or my parent founded a company, I spent my whole career growing the business with the thought that my children would run it, and they have no interest in doing so?"

Your reactions would likely be similar, extended to encompass the parental utterance, "Where did I go wrong?"

Fortunately or unfortunately, this situation is evolving into a trend that cannot be ignored.

The undeniable facts that surround the reality are:

- The children of owner/founders are oftentimes the beneficiaries of a terrific education.

- The children have likely had the opportunity to travel extensively both domestically and internationally.
- The children of Boomers have benefitted from the parental conditioning that results in feelings of confidence, experimentation, and encouragement to express oneself.
- The children of Boomers are not disposed to think of career decisions in the context of extended tenure.
- The children of owner/founders are not ungrateful, nor disrespectful. They are looking for different challenges in their careers.

There are, of course, exceptions to this emerging trend. However, the fact that there is an evolving narrative suggests the need to move beyond sentiment and towards strategic frameworks.

In **Discussion Partners'** Transition Advisory work in the Privately Held/Family Owned business sector, we have found that in 67% of the circumstances, a business has not been passed along to the next generation of family members.

Notwithstanding the unavoidable disappointment, the parent quickly realizes that this is, in fact, a tribute as their children have minds of their own.

The top five considerations as the owner transitions to the next steps encompass:

1. **Estate Planning**—development of a comprehensive plan that provides reassurance that wealth creation for the family has been secured
2. **Timing Determination**—The senior leader then has to determine how long they choose to stay involved.

In our experience, unless there are detracting circumstances, this is likely to be approximately three years.

3. **Growth Acceleration**—Often, the executive has a newfound energy concomitant with their now-extended tenure, focus on innovative strategic intents inclusive of new processes, products, and geographies.

4. **Transaction Contemplation**—Independent of potential buyer, employee, strategic, or investor, the executive focuses on a troika of refined initiatives inclusive of a) cleaning up of the balance sheet; b) raising the bar on performance; and c) replenishing the leadership population. All are transaction enhancers.

Saying "now what?" is understandable, but the "where did I go wrong?" assumption is not appropriate as you are by no means alone AND the fact that you raised independent children is a tribute to you.

**What is necessary is a purpose—built framework that predicts an alternative future for the company in tandem with an attitude of enjoy the ride!**

# Chapter 19
## Beware of Executive Coaches

**Discussion Partners** does periodic updates on Executive Coaching. The impetus for the first study was the feedback we had been receiving from our C-Suite clients about their satisfaction with the discipline and the value it added to their enterprise.

Our first study started shortly after the start of the global recession, when many displaced executives were forced to be in the market.

The headline from our initial study was, "It depends more on the coach than the circumstance."

The earliest research captured in detail the sentiments expressed and was featured in blogs and our 2013 book ***Executive Transition-Plotting The Opportunity!***

In our most recent study of over 400 CEOs, we found that not much had changed in the years since the initial posting.

The original study, with some interesting modifications, is offered for your information.

In the spirit of truth in advertising, the notification "**Beware of Dog**" should also apply to Executive Coaching.

The domain of Executive Coaching continues to grow rapidly for three independent reasons. Foremost, it has been well-researched and documented that the use of external coaches is the most-impactful of leadership development vehicles. The other two reasons: the displacement of many executives during the global recession and the escalating retirement of Boomer executives.

The more cynical of us remember the late '90s, when a displaced executive was going to start a dot.com. That aspiration has now been supplanted in many cases by well-intentioned but unprepared advisors who are now coaches.

It is doubtful one would feel comfortable being represented by a lawyer who hadn't been to law school or treated by a doctor who didn't attend medical school. So why do client sponsors feel more optimistic when they or their managers are being advised by someone whose credentials as a coach are primarily self-declaration as an expert?

The above is further complicated by the **Executive Coaching** industry lacking any regulatory oversight.

This updated Pulse Survey of our relationships changed the standard question from "To be an effective leader, what skills do you need?" to "What are the top five critical skills needed by an Executive Coach?"

**Top Five Responses**

- **Strong Business Fundamentals**—There is a need to be clear. Many coaches focus on advising on strategy and operations; others focus on leadership effectiveness. The response had more to do with the third area in that even when advising on the quality of a leadership bench, or correcting some less-then-attractive behaviors, there is a need for the coach to know enough about business to be credible with their client. *2019 update: Now more than ever, knowledge of global business and economics is a must.*

- **Sensei Tendencies**—The ability of the coach to weave in relevant war stories or lessons learned from their experience. At **Discussion Partners**, we refer to this as *Illustration Advisory.* There is, of course, the need to resist the temptation to pontificate, such as saying, "When I was a young manager …" *2019 update: CEOs are asking for an advanced script from the coach on how they intend to manage their client.*

- **Willingness to Confront**—The desire to avoid offending a client in order to preserve economic security can be taken too far in a relationship. There can be diplomatic ways to articulate, "What the hell were you thinking?" *2019 update: CEOs want to see more of this embedded in discourse, in many cases being the initial deliverer of bad news to the executive.*

- **Intellectual Curiosity**—This attribute initially surprised those of us at DPC, so shame on us! It is only logical that a client is entitled to expect that their advisor is staying current. Although the John Bordereaus, Noel Tichys, David Ulrichs, Jim Collins and Michael Porters of the world are in a class by themselves, the reputation of the coach can be enhanced if they share insights from others and their own documented points of view. *2019 update: CEO* *expect Coaches to have an organized fact-based point of view, preferably demonstrated through thought leadership.*

- **Willingness to Admit Failure**—Staying in a bad marriage is counterproductive if not counterintuitive. The same logic applies to a coaching relationship. If it isn't, working the coach should initiate the separation. Anything less is suboptimal for the client and an unfair position for an enterprise sponsor. *The 2019 update indicates that the time horizon for tolerating non-performance and/or bad behaviors is shortening.*

You will note that there is a presumption of a methodology and highly attuned interactive skills. Both are considered and continue to be based upon the 2019 update Threshold Attributes by CEOs.

Given the continued proliferation of those calling themselves Executive Coaches, the above is offered as a point of view to assist you in what DPC refers to as QQ (Qualification/Quality).

# Chapter 20
## Why Consider Transition Planning

Why is Transition Planning important? As the global economy continues to grow, the unemployment rate drops, and the need for experienced talent intensifies, two demographic issues need to be considered.

### 1) The Need to Embrace the Contribution of the Older Worker

*The Wall Street Journal* and *The Boston Globe* recently published articles addressing the challenges the legal profession faces in maintaining partners over a certain age. One article focused on an attorney who practiced, professionally and with support, until he was 96 years old. The second highlighted a 79-year-old partner who was challenging in court the position of his firm that he was "too old" to fulfill the obligations of being a partner. The article went on to speak about his actual productivity (among the highest-billing), scholarship (a regular contributor to legal journals and opinion pieces), and reputation as a mentor (younger and *middle-age* partners revere him as a mentor).

So beyond age …why this dilemma? His legacy firm stipulated that it was being prudent and needed to have a mandatory retirement age to make way for younger partners.

So, in the legal profession, as in the case of other sectors such as accounting, contribution is not a consideration. The main one is age! Hmmm.

Vitality is not a function of years. It is a function of preparation, outlook, health, intellectual curiosity, or just plain passion to continue doing what you know you do well.

Speaking of which …

## 2) The Need to Understand the Mental Model of the Younger Worker and the difference between Boomer Executives

Any survey of incoming college freshman will have interesting results in respect to generational differences. For example, in one survey, when asked, "Who was Michelangelo?" a response was "a computer virus." I thought this was obtuse until my wife explained to me that there is a computer virus called Michelangelo.

As Boomers, **DPC Partners** thought it would be interesting to create our own quiz and, just for fun, answer our own questions as if we were freshman (we wish!).

1. What was The Cold War? (One fought in the Arctic)
2. What was The Long March? (The first marathon)
3. Who was Beethoven? (A dog that starred in a couple of movies)
4. What was the Kitchen Debate? (An argument my parents had in the kitchen)
5. What was the Palmer Method? (The swing of an old golfer)

6. What is a Fountain Pen? (A fountain in the shape of a pen)
7. What is a Pop-Tart? (OK, this one is timeless)

The fact is, there is a wide range of knowledge, experience, and understanding between the Baby Boomers and Gen X or Y. This is not to say that one is better than the other but that, when combined, we have a depth and breadth of experience never before seen in the workforce. The question is how to combine the wisdom of age with the limited experience, yet boundless thirst for knowledge, of youth? And is relevance an issue of age, intellect, or exposure?

In reviewing the writings of Tammy Erickson and Lynda Gratton, the *WSJ* and *Globe* articles, recent studies, and, most importantly, my pro-Sistine Chapel response, I was thinking that maybe the idea that you lose it with age thing has some merit.

Nope. Regardless of age, all workers have the same desires:

1. The desire to be respected
2. The desire to be recognized
3. The desire to be mentored
4. The desire to be challenged
5. The desire for opportunity

The disconnect between the generations is not a function of age. There are more-accurate explanations.

The work **DPC** has been doing with transitioning executives since 2013, supported by our research and writing on the topic, have led to the inescapable conclusion that assisting executives in planning after they leave their organization is a sensible for the following reasons:

- Executives will have commercial involvement subsequent to their departures from their organization, and it is important that they feel supported.
- Organizations have the ability to proactively channel executive energies by avoiding distractions due to impending departure.
- The organizations' Human Capital functions have the ability to engender a reputation as progressive practitioners.

**The executives need to appreciate that their experience is their leverage in framing the next phase of their careers.**

# Chapter 21
## Is It Time For A Reset?

During our work with them, transitioning executives rarely discuss their plans without talking about the state of the world. The overarching sentiment is disappointment and the sincere desire that as they embark on new adventures, society and the world undergo a reset. In our client work, **Discussion Partners** is experiencing the same sense of disequilibrium.

As 2018 careened to an end, few would have disputed that it was a tumultuous year encompassing natural disasters, geo-political tensions, domestic polarization, and extreme positions on multiple matters.

Now, 2019 is not off to a great start.

In every aspect of daily life, we see an either/or mentality becoming prevalent: EITHER cats OR dogs. EITHER Republican OR Democrat. EITHER Citizen OR Foreigner. It's coffee or tea, and those who like both or prefer to drink water must pick a side or risk being excluded from the conversation.

In our client work, **DPC** has found these and other elements to be fostering an unfortunate and unintended consequence in the workplace environment. We are discerning a significant increase in the use of the words bully, victim, rude, and fear. During a recent **DPC** internal exercise focused on what are we noticing that is of concern, we concluded that these words are now normal.

The average age of **DPC** Advisors is now 67 with an on-average Consulting experience level of 40+ years, so when we notice such an observable trend, we have to ask, "What are the implications for our clients?" The conclusions we have drawn based upon this trend are three-fold:

1.  Many actions seem to prompt an overreaction: *reduction in filters, aka an epidemic of lack of restraint or perspective.*
2.  There is an expectation that, in order for someone to win, someone has to lose: *internal competition at the expense of collaboration as a team member or corporate member.*
3.  Biased listening is the communication foundation: *talking past each other, resulting in a loss of both objectivity and opportunities to learn.*

Our internal narrative has, regardless of personal or career situation, become built on underlying anxiety and driven by uncertainty. Accordingly, this disequilibrium is negatively influencing behavior and engagement and our perceptions of people, places, and even ideas, such as the issues of age and relevance the topics of this book.

During the Vietnam era, the saying "we have met the enemy and he is us" first surfaced in the comic strip *Pogo*. This sentiment was not US-centric and was being repeated in many societies.

Given the demographic of **DPC** Advisors and our Transition clients, our assertion is that this saying resonated due to societal circumstances. We believe a similar phenomenon is embedding within enterprise settings and, unless confronted, will be a lose/lose for the individual and the enterprise.

**History can repeat itself!**

# Chapter 22
# In Conclusion-Leveraging Experience To Address What's Next

Tammy Ericson, Ken Dychtwald, and Bob Morrison, in their McKinsey Award-winning *HBR* article ***It's Time To Retire Retirement*** and subsequent book ***Workforce Crisis***, asserted elegantly that Retirement is not a phase-down from relevance. Moreover, it is a platform for one to pursue alternative interests and avenues for personal satisfaction. Dr. Lynda Gratton, in her most-recent book ***The 100 Year Life***, affirms their research conclusions.

**Discussion Partners'** research and advisory interdictions reinforce their collective findings. Moreover, given the growth of the economy and emerging career opportunities, it is optimum to be mindful of how to channel personal and enterprise executive energies.

Thus **Discussion Partners'** overarching conclusion on the issue of Executive Transitions is two-fold:

1.  Enterprises, for a confluence of reasons, would be well served to support their transitioning executives as they ponder the question, "What's next?"

2. Executives in transition need to appreciate that their next steps as professionals will be the result of their willingness and ability to leverage their experience in the most-effective manner

On my next birthday as stated, I turn 70! I have had a great life with many fond memories. I am not a believer that getting old sucks. I know the alternative.

As a music lover, I appreciate The Beatles. In February 2014, there was a 50th Anniversary TV show about the night they appeared on *The Ed Sullivan Show*. Although the event was not celebrated as a national holiday, for those of us old enough to remember The Beatles' first appearance on *Ed Sullivan*, it does trigger memories and self-reflection. The fact that both Paul McCartney and Ringo Starr, in their late-70s, are still touring is emblematic of the lessons learned by **DPC** since 2013 and our internal narrative, "Getting old…bring it on!"

The increase in life expectancy, improved health, and the resulting continuation of an active lifestyle are all prompting Boomer executives to more seriously contemplate what they will do with their post-retirement time.

**DPC** provides Transition Coaching to executives and assists our clients in pre and post-employment planning. We have observed an emerging mental model executives employ in determining, "How will I spend my time?"

**The most important insight we have derived from our research and work is that fulfillment is more easily derived when the executive leverages the skills gained through experience and continue to use them in the next setting, such as:**

- **Type A Does Not Go Away**. The motivation that drives an executive to succeed does not disappear or decline appreciably when they leave the enterprise.
- **62 is the Catalyst Year**. Retiring Executives perceive this as the age that "if I ever wanted to do something else, now is the time." Obviously, this calls into question the wisdom of using 65 as the core year for most Succession Plans. For longer-tenured employees, this can also happen around age 50. Independent of which age is the pivot, the executive continues to pursue interests.
- **Different Does Not Mean A Job**. The desire of executives is not to join another company in a similar role. Alternatively, there is a focus on non-commercial ventures such as hobbies, philanthropy, and education.
- **The Portfolio Approach. DPC's** research and client experience align with the conclusion that executives identify a combination of 1) Commercial; 2) Board Membership; and 3) Self-Awareness (Improvement) PART-TIME initiatives in their planning model.

The question that also arises as we help executives plan is: What are the implications for the companies when Boomer executives are planning their retirement?

The need for corporate resources to assist executives in this planning process is emerging as an enterprise imperative. Anything less has potentially negative outcomes:

- The executive surprises the company by leaving in advance of the contemplated date
- Enterprise disruption as the executive becomes more distracted the closer they get to their departure date

- The lost opportunity to be recognized as a proactive employer, one that recognizes the disparate demands of the multi-generational workforce and plans accordingly

## Scary Additional Lessons Learned

In addition to the insights on the actual transitions derived from our client work with executives, we formed an additional conclusion: the ready-now candidates may not be as ready as we think!

Eighty-six percent of the executives in our 2013 pilot program for the launch of Transition Advisory services stipulated that their replacements were not as strong as they perceived them to be. *This sentiment has been borne out during our subsequent client work.*

Of course, when the sentiment was communicated, the tongue-in-cheek reaction was, "Of course you are irreplaceable!"

However, when we ask, "Why do you say that?" alignment remains in their responses regarding concerns:

- **Lack of Global Orientation**—For the most part, the next generation of executives are from the mid- to younger-Gen X age cohort. This group came of age when, due to multiple recessions, expatriate assignments and extensive international posts were curtailed if not outright eliminated.
- **Writing Skills**—This generation of managers are "PowerPoint aficionados who cannot write a complete paragraph," according to one senior executive. Although acknowledging this mode of communication is now standard, there is a perspective that it limits the cogency of an argument to a headline.

- **Collaboration Skills**—The sentiment expressed was that the next generation of executives "collaborates on-line at the expense of relationship building."
- **Intellectual Curiosity**—There is a perspective that the next generation of executives are subject-matter experts and focus on acquiring knowledge in their domain vs. securing a broader view driven by reading books on leadership of business leaders or biographies of political figures.

Our experience since 2013 has only solidified this perspective. The insights of these executives from different companies and diversified roles are persuasive.

These observations represent a reality that, if even close to accurate, suggest that the desires of executives to phase down concomitant to the enterprises' need to develop the next generation of leaders are more in intellectual synchronicity rather than practice.

In closing, and as the impetus to plan vs. react as an individual or enterprise, the Boomer mindset has shifted observably, as reinforced by the writing of thought leaders, the media, and **Discussion Partners'** research and client experience, from "what used to be?" to "what's next?" **Awareness of this evolution is of critical importance, dismissiveness of this reality is self-defeating.**

We prefer our clients not to become their own worst enemies. It is essential that they confront any aspect of the culture that nurtures anxiety, fear or disunity.

# Other Books by Tom Casey